Book 1:

Foundations of Strategic Experience Design

Master the Art of Creating Impactful Experiences: Practical Tools, Proven Strategies, and Cutting-Edge Technology for Novices, Transitioning Professionals, and Industry Leaders

Introduction: Experience Design – Shaping the Future of Interaction

In an era defined by digital transformation, the role of experience design (XD) has transcended its origins as a purely creative discipline. It has become a strategic force that shapes the way users interact with technology, brands, and services. Each touchpoint— whether an app, product, or customer interaction—offers the potential to craft a meaningful and lasting experience that harmonizes user needs with business objectives. Yet, the landscape is ever-evolving, driven by advances in artificial intelligence, data analytics, and automation. How can you stay ahead and ensure your designs remain relevant and impactful?

1

Foundations of Strategic Experience Design serves as your essential guide to not only mastering the principles of experience design but also navigating the shifting tides of technological innovation. Whether you're embarking on a new career, transitioning from another field, or seeking to elevate your current role, this book will equip you with the tools to stay current with emerging trends, harnessing technology as an enabler of creative excellence. Instead of reacting to the rapid pace of change, you'll learn how to proactively leverage AI, data, and other advancements to shape user experiences that resonate and deliver business value.

This is not merely a theoretical exploration; it is the culmination of years of hands-on experience leading multifunctional teams and managing multimillion-dollar engagements at the enterprise level. The strategies, frameworks, and insights shared in these pages are grounded in real-world results, offering you a blueprint for success that bridges the gap between user empathy and business growth.

Who Is This Book For?

1. Novices Beginning Their Journey into Experience Design

For those at the start of their careers, this book provides a foundation of essential principles, enabling you to make an immediate impact while continuing to evolve your expertise. From day one, you'll be equipped with practical techniques and insights that will help you deliver value to your employer or clients. But beyond the basics, you'll also learn how to approach emerging technologies—like AI and data-driven systems—with confidence, using them as tools to enhance your work and stay ahead in the ever-changing world of tech.

You'll discover how to:

- **Grasp the core concepts of experience design** and apply them effectively from your very first project.

- **Leverage technology** , using AI and data-driven insights to elevate your designs and improve business outcomes.
- **Set yourself on a path of growth** , building a skillset that evolves alongside the industry's technological advancements.

2. Transitioning Professionals

For those making a career shift, this book will serve as both a guide and a bridge—helping you understand the principles of experience design while seamlessly integrating your existing skills and expertise. You won't need to start from scratch. Instead, you'll learn how to adapt your current knowledge—whether in marketing, business, strategy, or another field—to the world of experience design, allowing you to bring a unique and valuable perspective. Additionally, you'll be introduced to key technologies, such as AI, that will position you as a forward-thinking leader in this new chapter of your career.
You'll learn how to:

- **Map your existing skills to experience design** , enhancing your transition and making it smoother and more impactful.
- **Harness emerging technologies** like AI and automation to enhance the depth and scope of your design solutions.
- **Position yourself as a leader** , using your past experience to inform innovative and user-centered design strategies.

3. Professionals Elevating Their Current Roles

If you're not planning to transition into a dedicated experience design role, this book still offers immense value. Whether you're in marketing, product development, engineering, or operations, the principles of experience design can help you elevate your current work and stand out in your organization. By integrating experience design methodologies and embracing new technologies, you'll be able to improve the outcomes of your projects, create more user-centered solutions, and stay competitive in a technology-driven marketplace.

You'll explore how to:

- **Infuse experience design into your current role** , creating more informed, user-centered strategies that drive business success.
- **Stay ahead of technological trends** , using tools like AI and data analytics to amplify your impact and elevate your work.
- **Unlock new areas of professional growth** , enhancing your skillset and positioning yourself as an invaluable asset to your team or organization.

Key Benefits of This Book

1. Proven, Real-World Approach

This book draws from years of direct experience leading large-scale experience design initiatives at the enterprise level. You'll gain insights into methodologies that have been tested, refined, and successfully applied across a range of industries. These strategies go beyond theory, offering you practical tools and frameworks that you can apply immediately, whether you're working on small projects or leading major transformations.

2. Balancing User Needs and Business Objectives

Experience design is about more than just creating beautiful interfaces. It's about crafting experiences that align with both the goals of the user and the objectives of the business. You'll learn how to strike this balance, ensuring that every design decision you make not only delights users but also drives measurable business results. Through this lens, you'll see how emerging technologies—

such as AI—can be harnessed to enrich user experiences while advancing strategic business goals.

3. Immediate Impact with Long-Term Growth

From the moment you start reading, this book equips you with the foundational knowledge you need to make an immediate impact. You'll learn how to approach your projects with the right mindset and techniques to contribute effectively from day one. But it doesn't stop there—this book also sets you on a path for continuous learning and development, helping you evolve as the field of experience design grows alongside technological advancements.

4. Staying Ahead of Technological Change

Technology is at the heart of modern experience design, and this book will guide you on how to stay ahead of its rapid evolution. Whether it's AI, data-driven insights, or new design tools, you'll learn how to leverage these technologies to your advantage, positioning yourself as a proactive innovator in your field rather than a follower of trends. This ability to harness technology will help you maintain control over your work and consistently deliver cutting-edge experiences.

What Makes This Book Different?

Foundations of Strategic Experience Design offers a unique blend of practical, real-world strategies with a forward-thinking approach to technology. While many books on experience design focus on theory, this one bridges the gap between strategic vision and hands-on execution, helping you craft experiences that are both impactful and measurable.

Moreover, this book goes beyond the basics to explore both the **hard skills** —such as research, prototyping, and design execution—and the **soft skills** —like collaboration, facilitation, and storytelling—that are essential for success in today's tech-centric world. You'll not only learn how to design great experiences, but also how to build, sell, and position them to create lasting value in the market. With insights that span product development, service design, and enterprise-level transformations, this book is your roadmap to becoming a leader in experience design.

Start Your Journey

The field of experience design is a journey—one that promises to reshape how you think about products, services, and user interactions. Whether you're stepping into this world for the first time, transitioning from another discipline, or looking to enhance your current role, **Foundations of Strategic Experience Design** will guide you every step of the way.

This book will not only equip you with the knowledge and tools to create immediate value, but it will also help you cultivate a mindset that balances creativity with strategy, user empathy with business acumen, and cutting-edge technology with timeless design principles. As you embark on this journey, you'll gain the skills needed to master experience design, while also learning how to stay ahead of industry changes and lead with confidence.

The future of experience design is yours to shape. Are you ready to begin?

Chapter 1: Why Experience Design Matters

Introduction

Experience design (XD) is omnipresent in today's world, shaping every aspect of how we engage with products, services, and brands. From the moment we wake up and check our phones to the time we order food, use transportation, or communicate with colleagues, XD influences our interactions with everything around us. It's no longer just a matter of aesthetics or usability—experience design impacts the very fabric of businesses, dictating how they are perceived and whether they succeed or fail.

In this chapter, we will explore the broad reach of XD, focusing on how it has evolved from its origins in graphic design and human-computer interaction (HCI) into a critical strategic asset for businesses. Through examples from the tech, automotive, aviation, and manufacturing industries, we'll highlight how thoughtful experience design creates competitive differentiation, fosters loyalty, and drives long-term business success. Additionally, we will delve into the psychology behind how humans make decisions and how XD affects user behavior, from initial impressions to sustained loyalty.

We will also address the challenges of designing experiences in complex industries where factors such as physics, regulations, supply chain issues, and technical constraints must all be balanced. By the end of this chapter, you will have a comprehensive understanding of why XD is essential for both users and businesses, as well as a glimpse of the in-depth frameworks and methodologies that will be covered in the chapters that follow.

1.1 Experience Design in Everyday Life

In the modern world, experience design is not only a concept for digital products but a force that shapes everyday life. Whether it's ordering food through a mobile app, interacting with customer service, or even navigating physical spaces, the design of these experiences impacts how smoothly, effectively, and pleasantly our daily activities unfold.

Take, for example, the world of **transportation** . Ride-sharing apps like **Uber** and **Lyft** have revolutionized urban mobility. At first glance, it seems the primary value of these apps lies in convenience—getting a ride with just a few taps on a screen. But the success of these platforms runs much deeper. The experience they create is not just about calling a car but about the transparency of the driver's profile, the ability to track the ride, seamless payments, and even rating the driver. Each of these elements, carefully designed, builds trust and comfort for users who may have once been hesitant to step into a stranger's car.

Experience design also goes beyond technology and enters our physical spaces. Consider the environment created by **Starbucks** . The coffeehouse chain is not only selling beverages; it's selling an atmosphere, a consistent experience across all of its global locations. The way the stores are designed—from the warm lighting to the communal seating—encourages customers to stay longer, to work, or socialize, all of which are intentional design choices that build customer loyalty. It's a subtle experience that elevates Starbucks above simply being a place to grab a coffee.

Human Experience as the Focus: In many successful products, users don't notice the intricacies of design because it works so well that it becomes invisible. This is known as the **non-experience** : an interaction that feels so natural that the user hardly thinks about it at all. Think about how **Apple** products work seamlessly together. When you open your MacBook, your iPhone automatically connects to share photos or files via AirDrop without you needing to configure anything. This level of integration is a masterclass in experience design, making technology feel like an extension of the user's daily life. For many users, the technology fades into the background, and the focus is purely on the experience itself.

1.2 The Business Impact of Experience Design

Experience design isn't just about creating user-friendly products— it's about crafting interactions that resonate with people on an emotional level, leading to stronger business performance. Companies that understand the importance of XD consistently outperform their competitors in terms of customer loyalty, revenue growth, and market share.

Apple has long been recognized for its user-centered design, which prioritizes simplicity and elegance in every product. Apple's devices are easy to use, intuitive, and aesthetically pleasing. But it's the cohesive experience that truly sets the company apart. Whether you're using an iPhone, a MacBook, or an Apple Watch, the experience feels unified, and that's no accident. This level of consistency builds trust with users, leading to fierce customer loyalty even in the face of strong competition. Despite the rise of other smartphone makers offering comparable or superior hardware, Apple users remain devoted, often purchasing the latest iteration of the iPhone year after year.

Amazon is another company that has mastered experience design as a business strategy. Its one-click ordering system, personalized recommendations, and efficient delivery options are all designed to make shopping as frictionless as possible. Amazon has set the bar so high in terms of user expectations that it has become the gold standard for e-commerce. Competitors that fail to match this level of convenience often struggle to maintain market share.

The Cost of Poor Design: The consequences of ignoring XD can be dire. **Blockbuster** is a well-known example of a company that fell behind because it failed to adapt its customer experience to changing consumer preferences. As customers flocked to streaming services like **Netflix** , Blockbuster clung to its traditional rental model, not recognizing how the experience of consuming media had fundamentally changed. By the time Blockbuster tried to pivot, it was too late. Netflix, with its sleek, user-friendly streaming interface, had already won over the market.

In the next chapters, we will dive deeper into how experience design frameworks can help businesses avoid the fate of companies like Blockbuster by continuously adapting and refining their user experiences to stay ahead of the curve.

1.3 Human Psychology and Experience Design

At the core of every interaction between a product and its user is psychology. Humans are wired to make decisions quickly, often forming opinions about a product or service within seconds of their first interaction. These initial impressions can have a lasting impact on how users perceive a brand, influencing whether they continue to engage with it or abandon it for a competitor.

First Impressions Matter: When a user downloads an app or visits a website, their first few moments interacting with it are critical. If the app is slow, if the interface is confusing, or if the experience is cumbersome, users will quickly abandon it and form a negative perception of the entire brand. On the other hand, a smooth and intuitive first experience can create a positive impression that encourages further engagement. This is why companies like **Google** focus heavily on the speed and simplicity of their products.

Google's search engine, for instance, is designed to deliver instant results, minimizing any barriers to finding information.

Tesla is another great example of how first impressions drive user perception. Tesla's minimalistic car interiors, large touchscreens, and advanced self-driving features create an immediate sense of futuristic design and ease of use. This seamless experience isn't just about driving—it's about making users feel like they're part of something innovative and cutting-edge. From the first test drive to the ownership experience, every interaction with Tesla is designed to build loyalty and excitement.

In the following chapters, we will delve into specific psychological principles that inform good experience design, such as cognitive load, emotion-driven design, and the psychology of choice, all of which are essential to understanding how users form long-term attachments to products and services.

1.4 The Complexity of Designing for Industries

In some industries, experience design goes beyond digital interfaces and aesthetics to address real-world complexities such as physics, safety, regulatory requirements, and supply chain logistics. Designing something like a smartphone or an app is one thing, but designing experiences for transportation, aviation, or manufacturing requires a completely different set of considerations.

Aviation: When designing a new aircraft, companies like **Boeing** or **Airbus** face the challenge of balancing passenger comfort with stringent safety standards, fuel efficiency, and operational reliability. The seating arrangement, cabin layout, lighting, and in-flight entertainment systems must all contribute to an experience that satisfies both passengers and airline operators. At the same time, these design choices are constrained by physics—the need to maximize aerodynamic efficiency and minimize weight. Even the smallest design decisions, such as the width of the seats or the placement of overhead bins, can have a significant impact on how passengers perceive their journey.

Aircraft design also involves considerations around **supply chains** and **maintenance** . If an aircraft is designed in a way that makes certain parts difficult to access or replace, it can lead to costly delays for airlines. Designers must, therefore, collaborate with engineers, mechanics, and supply chain experts to ensure that the product is not only comfortable and safe but also operationally efficient.

Automotive Industry: Similarly, experience design plays a crucial role in the **automotive industry** . When designing a car, manufacturers must consider everything from **aerodynamics** to **driver safety** , **fuel efficiency** , and **comfort** . Car companies like **BMW** and **Tesla** have mastered the art of combining engineering precision with a luxurious driving experience. Tesla, in particular, has disrupted the traditional car-buying process by offering an entirely digital sales experience. Customers can customize and purchase their cars online, and over-the-air software updates ensure that the user experience continues to improve long after the purchase.

In industries like aviation and automotive manufacturing, design decisions are not only about aesthetics—they are about balancing user needs with complex, behind-the-scenes factors such as supply chains, engineering constraints, and regulatory requirements. This intersection of design and operational complexity will be explored further in the upcoming chapters as we introduce frameworks for collaborative experience design that can be applied to industries beyond tech.

1.5 The Future of Experience Design: Technology and Human-Centric Innovation

As we look toward the future, experience design will continue to be a driving force behind innovation, especially as new technologies like **artificial intelligence (AI)** , **machine learning... (AI)** , and **machine learning (ML)** become even more integrated into our daily lives. In particular, AI-driven experiences, such as virtual assistants or recommendation algorithms, will present new challenges and opportunities for designers. The goal of future experience design will be to humanize these technologies, ensuring that they remain intuitive, empathetic, and user-friendly rather than alienating or overwhelming users.

Consider the rise of **Amazon Alexa** and **Google Assistant** —two AI-powered virtual assistants that have made conversational interfaces mainstream. While these systems are driven by complex algorithms, their success hinges on how natural and effortless the interaction feels to the user. Experience designers work to ensure that these interactions feel human, that the AI understands context, and that the system feels helpful rather than robotic. As AI continues to evolve, experience design will be crucial in guiding how these technologies fit into our lives.

Another emerging area of focus for experience designers is the **Internet of Things (IoT)** . Imagine a world where your home, car, and workplace are all connected in an intelligent ecosystem, where everything from your lighting to your thermostat automatically adjusts to your preferences. While the technology to make this possible is rapidly advancing, the challenge for designers is to ensure that this interconnected world remains easy to use and doesn't overwhelm users with complexity. The future of experience design will involve crafting seamless, frictionless interactions that make these smart environments feel intuitive and helpful rather than cumbersome.

In the upcoming chapters, we will explore how experience designers can harness the power of AI and IoT to create human-centered experiences that anticipate user needs and enhance everyday life. We will also discuss the ethical implications of designing for AI, ensuring that these systems remain transparent, trustworthy, and inclusive.

1.6 Conclusion: Experience Design as a Business Imperative

Throughout this chapter, we've explored why experience design matters—not just as a tool for creating visually appealing products, but as a core driver of business success, customer loyalty, and technological innovation. In today's competitive landscape, companies that fail to prioritize XD risk falling behind, while those that invest in creating seamless, intuitive experiences are reaping the rewards of stronger customer engagement, brand loyalty, and long-term growth.

From everyday interactions like ordering coffee at **Starbucks** or booking a ride on **Uber** , to more complex systems like **aircraft design** and **automotive engineering** , experience design shapes how we perceive and interact with the world. It is a powerful force that drives business strategy, transforms customer experiences, and creates lasting emotional connections between users and brands.

As we move into the next chapters, we will dive deeper into the practical tools and methodologies that enable businesses to implement effective experience design. You will learn about journey mapping, prototyping, and the critical role of user feedback in shaping and refining experiences. These foundational tools will give you the skills to not only improve the user experience but also to align these experiences with your business goals for measurable success.

Experience design is no longer a luxury—it is a necessity for any business looking to thrive in the digital age. Let's explore how to leverage its full potential in the chapters to come.

Chapter 2: The Basics of Experience Design

Introduction: The Experience Spectrum – A Continuum and a Process

Experience design (XD) isn't a static or one-time task—it's a continuous, evolving journey that spans across multiple phases, forming what we call the **experience spectrum** . The experience spectrum represents the entire lifecycle of creating and refining an experience, from setting the vision and strategy, through research and prototyping, to validation and ongoing innovation. It is both a continuum—where each phase feeds into the next—and a cyclical process, where constant refinement and iteration are necessary to keep pace with evolving user needs and business goals.

This chapter will dive deeply into the experience spectrum, exploring each phase in detail, from **vision setting** to **continuous validation**. Along the way, we will highlight both the **technical tools** and **hands-on techniques** required to implement each phase, as well as the **collaborative, alignment-driven methods** needed to ensure everyone from stakeholders to users remains engaged, represented, and aligned. We'll show you how to navigate the spectrum to deliver value incrementally while staying focused on long-term vision.

2.1 The Experience Spectrum: A Continuum and Process

The **experience spectrum** encapsulates the holistic process of designing a product or service that delivers meaningful value to users while advancing the goals of the business. This is why it's described as both a **continuum** and a **cyclical process** :

- **Continuum:** Each step in the experience spectrum—starting with strategy, moving through research, experience architecture, experience design, and ending with validation and iteration—flows naturally from one phase to the next. The knowledge and insights gained at each step inform the subsequent phases.
- **Cyclical Process:** At the same time, the experience spectrum is inherently iterative. User needs evolve, market dynamics shift, and technology advances. As a result, businesses must continually revisit earlier phases in the process, refining their approach based on feedback, data, and changing conditions.

This approach enables businesses to maintain long-term vision while delivering incremental value—each phase of the spectrum contributes to short-term gains (such as ROI) without losing sight of the bigger picture. Let's walk through each phase of the experience spectrum, illustrating how it works in practice.

2.2 Vision Setting and Strategy: Defining the North Star

The experience spectrum begins with a clear vision and strategy. This phase is all about aligning business objectives with user needs and setting a long-term direction—often referred to as the **North Star** —that will guide the project through each phase. At this stage, it's critical to bring all stakeholders together to define what success looks like.

Hands-on Techniques:

- **Vision Workshops:** These are structured sessions where stakeholders across different departments collaborate to define the long-term vision of the project. Using tools like **empathy maps** , **value proposition canvases** , and **SWOT analysis** , these workshops help build consensus and ensure that the vision addresses both business goals and user needs.
- **Jobs to Be Done (JTBD):** This framework helps teams focus on the core problems users are trying to solve, rather than simply designing features. JTBD can be used to clearly articulate the motivations behind user behavior and align the design strategy with these deeper goals. For example, instead of focusing on how to build a faster coffee machine, JTBD asks why users need coffee quickly—perhaps it's about increasing productivity, creating more leisure time, or offering comfort in the morning.

Collaboration and Alignment Techniques:

- **Stakeholder Alignment Sessions:** To align all teams, regular sessions that bring together business leaders, designers, engineers, and marketers are crucial. These sessions foster a shared understanding of goals and constraints and help resolve potential conflicts in priorities early on.
- **Empathy Mapping:** Creating empathy maps with stakeholders not only ensures that the user's needs are represented but also promotes a shared understanding of the emotional drivers that will guide design decisions. This collaborative exercise breaks down silos, ensuring that teams understand both the user's perspective and the business objectives.

Example Scenario:
Imagine a company setting out to redesign its customer support system. In the vision-setting phase, the company might hold a **vision workshop** to determine the ultimate goal—streamlined support interactions that reduce user frustration and cut operational costs. The **JTBD** method would then help the team understand why users are seeking support in the first place—whether they need help resolving technical issues or simply clarifying how to use a product more effectively.

2.3 Research: Uncovering Insights and User Needs

Once the vision is set, it's time to dive into **user research** . This phase aims to uncover deep insights about users—their behaviors, needs, pain points, and expectations. It also involves market research to understand competitive landscapes and trends.

Hands-on Techniques:

- **User Interviews and Surveys:** Direct interviews and surveys help gather qualitative data from real users. By asking open-ended questions, researchers can gain insights into how users currently experience the product or service, what frustrates them, and what delights them. This helps inform the next phase, where we start to map these insights into experience architecture.
- **Journey Mapping:** This technique visualizes the steps users take when interacting with a product or service. It identifies key touchpoints, pain points, and opportunities for improvement. For example, a journey map for an online banking app might reveal that users find the authentication process frustrating, leading to drop-offs before completing transactions.

Collaboration and Alignment Techniques:

- **Co-Creation Workshops:** These sessions bring users, stakeholders, and design teams together to brainstorm potential solutions. This approach ensures that user voices are heard early in the process and helps align internal teams with user insights. Co-creation workshops are particularly effective when working on complex or high-stakes products where user needs and business objectives may conflict.

Example Scenario:
A company looking to redesign its e-commerce website might conduct **user interviews** to understand why customers abandon their carts. Through these interviews, the company learns that users find the checkout process too complicated and prefer payment options like Apple Pay, which are not currently supported. This

research directly informs the next phases of architecture and design.

2.4 Experience Architecture: Translating Vision into Actionable Plans

With research insights in hand, the next phase is to translate those findings into a **blueprint** for the user experience—this is where **experience architecture** comes into play. In this phase, teams structure how the user will interact with the product, ensuring that the entire journey is cohesive, seamless, and intuitive.

Hands-on Techniques:

- **Information Architecture (IA):** IA focuses on organizing and structuring content in a way that is logical and intuitive for users. This could involve creating site maps for digital experiences or interaction flows for physical products. The goal is to ensure that users can easily find the information they need and navigate the experience without frustration.
- **Wireframing:** Wireframes are low-fidelity representations of the experience, used to map out the layout and structure before moving into detailed design. They allow teams to focus on the flow and functionality of the experience without getting bogged down in visual details. Wireframing is a critical step in validating the overall architecture and gaining feedback from stakeholders early in the process.

Collaboration and Alignment Techniques:

- **Experience Mapping Workshops:** These workshops bring cross-functional teams together to create experience maps, which help visualize the user's journey across all touchpoints. By getting stakeholders involved in this process, companies ensure that design decisions are aligned with both user needs and business objectives.
- **Card Sorting:** This technique is used during the IA phase to involve users in how information should be categorized and labeled. By asking users to organize content into logical categories, designers can ensure that the experience architecture reflects real-world user behavior, reducing confusion and improving usability.

Example Scenario:
Imagine redesigning a hospital's patient portal. The **information architecture** process might reveal that patients have trouble finding their test results because they are buried under irrelevant menus. Using **wireframes** , the team can create a simpler navigation system that surfaces important information more intuitively.

2.5 Prototyping and Validation: Bringing Ideas to Life

Prototyping is where the concepts and architecture begin to take tangible form. This phase is all about translating ideas into testable solutions, refining them through iteration, and validating them with real users.

Hands-on Techniques:

- **Rapid Prototyping:** Rapid prototypes allow teams to quickly test design ideas without investing significant time or resources. Tools like Sketch, Figma, or even paper prototypes are useful here, as they allow for quick feedback and iteration.
- **Usability Testing:** Once a prototype is built, usability testing allows teams to observe real users interacting with the design. This phase is crucial for identifying usability issues and ensuring that the product is intuitive. Usability testing can be done in-person or remotely, depending on the scope of the project.

Collaboration and Alignment Techniques:

- **Design Sprints:** A design sprint is a time-constrained process where teams focus on solving a critical design challenge. This collaborative technique involves multiple iterations of prototyping and feedback within a short time frame. It brings stakeholders, designers, and users together to work intensely on refining the solution.
- **A/B Testing:** This technique involves comparing two versions of a product to determine which performs better. For example, a company may test two different layouts for a homepage to see which one leads to higher conversion rates. A/B testing not only validates design choices but also provides measurable insights into what resonates with users.

Example Scenario:
A company redesigning its customer support interface might develop several **prototypes** for the new chatbot functionality. By running **usability tests** , the team discovers that users find one design too impersonal, while another design leads to quicker issue

resolution. Based on this feedback, the company iterates on the chatbot design, balancing user preferences for...resolving issues quickly and maintaining a personalized feel, the business continues to refine the chatbot's user interface.

2.6 Continuous Validation and Innovation: Ensuring Growth and Adaptability

Once the product is live, the work isn't over—continuous validation and innovation are essential to ensuring that the product evolves with user needs and business goals. This final phase focuses on using data, feedback, and new technologies to iterate on the design and push the boundaries of what's possible.

Hands-on Techniques:

- **A/B Testing and Multivariate Testing:** Once a product is launched, continuous optimization can be achieved through A/B testing and multivariate testing. By constantly comparing different versions of key features (like buttons, forms, or workflows), businesses can refine the user experience and maximize conversion rates. This approach ensures that the design is always improving based on real-world data.
- **Data Analytics and Heatmaps:** By using tools like Google Analytics or heatmap software, teams can track how users interact with a product. These insights allow teams to identify areas where users struggle or drop off and make improvements based on actual behavior. For example, a company may discover that users are not scrolling down to see important information on a landing page, leading them to redesign the page layout.

Collaboration and Alignment Techniques:

- **Feedback Loops with Users:** Regular user feedback sessions—whether through surveys, interviews, or direct usability tests—help teams stay connected with real user needs. These sessions ensure that design decisions are always informed by actual user behavior and preferences, making the product more responsive and adaptive over time.
- **Innovation Sprints:** Similar to design sprints, innovation sprints are focused on exploring and testing new ideas for future iterations. These sprints may focus on integrating emerging technologies, like AI or machine learning, or on exploring entirely new features that could drive long-term growth.

Example Scenario:
A streaming platform like **Netflix** might use **A/B testing** to experiment with different designs for its home screen, testing whether certain layouts lead to higher viewer engagement. By analyzing **heatmaps** and data analytics, the platform could determine which content arrangements keep users watching longer, driving continuous improvement while maintaining alignment with business objectives.

2.7 Conclusion: The Experience Spectrum as a Strategic Asset

The **experience spectrum** represents a comprehensive and iterative approach to experience design, starting from strategy and vision, moving through research, architecture, design, and validation, and culminating in continuous improvement and innovation. It's a process that prioritizes user needs while driving incremental business value at every stage.

As we move forward through the remaining chapters, we will dive deeper into how specific tools and methods discussed here, like **prototyping**, **journey mapping**, and **A/B testing**, can be applied across different industries and project scopes. You'll learn how to balance the need for continuous innovation with the imperative to deliver tangible business results, and how to leverage experience design as a critical driver of both user satisfaction and business success.

Chapter 3: Experience Design Strategy – Aligning User Needs with Business Goals

Introduction: Why Experience Design Strategy Matters

Experience design (XD) has evolved from a design function to a strategic asset that drives both customer satisfaction and business success. It's not just about creating beautiful interfaces; it's about creating experiences that resonate with users on a deeper level, align with business objectives, and contribute to long-term growth. Effective XD strategy means understanding the needs of users and the goals of the business, then using experience design to connect the two in a way that drives measurable results.

In this chapter, we'll explore how experience design functions as a central component of business strategy, influencing everything from customer acquisition and retention to brand loyalty and revenue growth. Through tools like journey mapping, empathy mapping, and alignment workshops, experience design strategy becomes more than a creative endeavor—it becomes a structured approach to driving business outcomes. We'll examine each of these tools in detail, showing how they can be used to align user needs with business goals across different phases of the experience spectrum.

3.1 The Role of Experience Design in Business Strategy

Experience design is a powerful tool for businesses looking to differentiate themselves in today's competitive landscape. When experience design aligns with business goals, it becomes a crucial part of a company's strategy, influencing everything from product development to brand perception. Experience design offers more than just a set of design principles; it serves as a guide for aligning a company's entire ecosystem—engineering, marketing, customer service, and operations—around the user.

Building the Connection Between User Needs and Business Goals

When XD is incorporated into business strategy, it transforms how companies approach product development and user engagement. Take, for example, a subscription-based app. If a company prioritizes user retention, the XD strategy would focus on reducing friction during onboarding, simplifying the user journey, and delivering ongoing value through personalized experiences. Each design decision made with this strategy reinforces both user satisfaction and business growth.

Incorporating XD into the business strategy also helps companies to innovate and stay relevant. By consistently aligning design decisions with user feedback, companies can identify new opportunities to enhance user experience, leading to increased engagement, loyalty, and brand advocacy. **Apple** , for example, has used XD as a business strategy by prioritizing simplicity, ease of use, and intuitive design across all its products. The cohesive experience they provide has led to an almost unparalleled level of customer loyalty.

3.2 Crafting a Holistic Experience Design Strategy

A robust XD strategy must be holistic, addressing every touchpoint in the user journey and aligning them with the company's broader goals. This is not about focusing solely on isolated features; instead, it's about ensuring a consistent, meaningful experience across the entire lifecycle of the user's relationship with the product or service.

The User Journey as a Matrix of Stages and Depths

The user journey is best understood as a **matrix of stages and depths** that tracks both the linear progression of the user's experience (e.g., awareness, engagement, retention) and the varying degrees of interaction depth (e.g., informational, functional, emotional). By viewing the journey in this way, companies can identify critical stages where user needs align with business priorities, allowing them to tailor their experience design efforts accordingly.

For example, the **onboarding process** is a critical stage for subscription-based services. A poorly designed onboarding experience can lead to high drop-off rates, negatively impacting customer acquisition costs and retention. By mapping out this specific stage in detail, companies can identify opportunities to streamline and personalize the onboarding experience, ensuring new users understand the value of the product and are more likely to stay engaged.

Real-World Example:
Consider a SaaS company launching a project management tool. Using the matrix approach, they might identify that users frequently abandon the onboarding process because they feel overwhelmed by the number of features. By focusing on onboarding as a distinct stage and simplifying the first few interactions, they can help users feel competent quickly, which aligns with both the business goal of user retention and the user's need for clarity and ease.

3.3 Tools and Techniques for Building an Experience Design Strategy

To implement a successful experience design strategy, it's essential to use the right mix of tools and techniques. Here, we'll break down the tools into two main categories: **hands-on techniques** that directly shape the user experience and **collaborative techniques** that build alignment within the organization.

Hands-On Techniques

1. Journey Mapping and Experience Blueprints

Journey mapping is one of the foundational tools in experience design strategy. It visualizes the end-to-end experience of the user, from initial awareness through to post-purchase engagement, helping identify where the business can enhance the user's journey to align with strategic goals. Experience blueprints take this a step further by documenting each phase in detail, specifying the goals, pain points, and expected outcomes for each touchpoint.

Example:

For a luxury travel company, a journey map could reveal that customers often feel frustrated when arranging personalized travel itineraries. By using an experience blueprint, the company can detail each phase—from booking to post-trip follow-up—ensuring every touchpoint is optimized to reduce stress, provide clarity, and align with the brand's goal of offering a seamless, high-end experience.

2. Rapid Prototyping and Usability Testing

Rapid prototyping allows teams to quickly test design concepts, gather feedback, and iterate on ideas before investing in full development. This technique is particularly valuable in validating design assumptions and ensuring alignment with business objectives early on.

Usability testing complements rapid prototyping by observing real users as they interact with the prototype. Testing early and often

26

allows teams to make data-driven decisions, ensuring that the final product is both intuitive and aligned with user expectations.

Example:
A financial services app might prototype different layouts for a dashboard. Through usability testing, the team discovers that users prefer a simple, consolidated view rather than detailed financial data. This insight directly informs the design, ensuring that users feel empowered and engaged, leading to increased app usage and improved customer retention.

Collaborative Techniques

1. Vision Alignment Workshops
Vision alignment workshops are sessions that bring together key stakeholders from design, engineering, marketing, and management to define the strategic vision. These workshops help align the team around a shared goal, ensuring that everyone has a clear understanding of what the experience is meant to achieve and how it supports the broader business objectives.

In these workshops, stakeholders work together to outline the key objectives of the experience, aligning both user and business goals. The collaborative nature of these sessions helps reduce silos and ensures that all team members feel a sense of ownership over the strategy, leading to more cohesive and effective design.

Example:
A telecommunications company looking to launch a new app may conduct a vision alignment workshop to define what success looks like. This could include metrics such as daily active users, reduced support calls, and increased customer satisfaction. By setting clear objectives across departments, the entire team understands the importance of designing an app that is both functional and user-friendly.

2. Empathy Mapping and Co-Creation Sessions
Empathy mapping is a tool used to understand users' thoughts, feelings, and pain points. It enables teams to gain a more nuanced understanding of the user's perspective, helping to create a design strategy that addresses real needs. Co-creation sessions, where

users collaborate with designers to brainstorm solutions, are another way to ensure that the final design reflects genuine user input.

Example:

In the automotive industry, empathy mapping could reveal that drivers feel stressed about the complexity of in-car infotainment systems. A co-creation session with drivers would then allow designers to explore ideas with direct user input, helping to design an interface that is more intuitive and minimizes distraction.

3.4 Aligning Experience Design with Business Goals: Defining and Measuring Success

A crucial aspect of experience design strategy is establishing clear, measurable goals that align with business outcomes. Experience design should be seen as a performance-driven function, where every design decision is evaluated based on its impact on key performance indicators (KPIs) that reflect user engagement and business success.

Key Metrics and How to Use Them:

- **Customer Lifetime Value (CLV):** This measures the total revenue a customer generates over their relationship with the company. Improving CLV often involves optimizing the user experience to increase engagement and retention.
- **Net Promoter Score (NPS):** This measures customer loyalty by asking users how likely they are to recommend the product to others. A higher NPS typically reflects a positive user experience, while a lower score signals areas for improvement.
- **Conversion Rates and Engagement Metrics:** These metrics help track how effectively users progress through the funnel or use the product, such as from a trial version to a paid subscription.

Example:
A subscription service may focus on CLV as its primary KPI. By creating an experience design strategy focused on user satisfaction during the trial period, they can increase the likelihood of conversion to a paid plan, thereby improving CLV.

3.5 Experience Design as a Driver of Long-Term Growth

Experience design, when strategically integrated, has the potential to drive long-term business growth. It's about building meaningful relationships with users, creating experiences that foster loyalty and advocacy, and continuously improving based on data and feedback.
Example:
Tesla has changed the landscape of the automotive industry not only through its electric vehicle technology but through a design-centric approach that keeps customers engaged long after their initial purchase. Regular software updates, a unique sales model, and a forward-thinking approach to the driving experience have built a devoted customer base that actively promotes the brand. Tesla's approach demonstrates how an experience-focused strategy can be a long-term growth driver.

In the **luxury market**, companies like Rolex understand that buying a luxury watch is more than a transaction—it's an experience that ties into status, legacy, and personal expression. Every touchpoint, from the store environment to post-purchase support, reinforces the brand's commitment to quality and exclusivity. This deep connection with the customer enhances long-term brand loyalty and customer lifetime value.

3.6 Conclusion: Integrating Experience Design into Business Strategy

Experience design is more than a design process; it's a business strategy that, when done right, elevates customer satisfaction, strengthens brand loyalty, and drives long-term growth. By aligning XD with business goals, companies can ensure that every design decision contributes to the larger strategic objectives, from improving customer retention to enhancing brand reputation.
As we continue through the book, we'll delve deeper into methodologies for embedding experience design into company workflows and breaking down silos to create cross-functional alignment. By integrating experience design at every level, you'll learn how to drive both continuous improvement and measurable results. Experience design, when viewed as a strategic asset, can be the key to achieving sustainable growth, setting your business apart in today's competitive landscape, and creating products and services that genuinely resonate with users.
This comprehensive approach to experience design strategy, combining user-centered thinking with business alignment, will be foundational as we explore more advanced techniques for embedding experience design into organizational processes in the following chapters.

Chapter 4: Mapping User Journeys – From Strategy to Detailed Interaction

Introduction: The Strategic Value of Mapping User Journeys
Mapping user journeys is a foundational element in experience design, linking the high-level vision of a business to the detailed, tactical interactions users experience. A user journey is a strategic tool that provides traceability, connecting every user interaction to broader business goals. When effectively mapped, user journeys become a blueprint that not only defines where value is delivered but also validates its impact. Each touchpoint, no matter how small,

drives progress toward the overarching goal, ensuring alignment across teams and clarity of purpose.

In this chapter, we'll explore how user journeys maximize business value by building a solid foundation for understanding, defining problems, and guiding interactions. We'll also discuss how journey mapping connects strategic and tactical layers, helping businesses retrace every interaction to core objectives. With real-world examples, we'll see how user journeys are used in contexts like service design, customer experience, and marketing to deliver measurable outcomes and create a cohesive experience from start to finish.

4.1 Understanding the User Journey as a Matrix: Connecting Strategy to Tactics

A user journey is best understood as a **matrix** of **stages** and **levels** . Each stage represents a step in the user's journey (from awareness to decision-making), while the levels capture the depth of engagement and interaction. This matrix approach allows businesses to view the user journey as a continuum that goes beyond individual interactions, linking tactical actions to the broader strategic vision of the company.

In mapping user journeys, this matrix format enables businesses to identify, isolate, and optimize each stage and interaction. The journey becomes a blueprint, showing how each minor detail contributes to long-term business objectives. This perspective is particularly valuable in aligning tactical-level details, like the wording on a checkout button, with strategic goals, such as increasing conversion rates and enhancing brand perception.

Example: SaaS Onboarding Process

Consider a software-as-a-service (SaaS) platform aimed at small businesses. In the user journey matrix, the onboarding process might represent a critical stage. At this stage, the goal is to ensure users understand the product's value and feel comfortable navigating the interface. By mapping each touchpoint in the onboarding journey—from account setup to completing a first task—

the company can track how every interaction (such as a tooltip or welcome email) reinforces the overarching goal of user retention and satisfaction.

Through this journey, each detail, such as the clarity of instructional content or the availability of support, nudges the user forward. An improvement as simple as rewording tooltips or adding an onboarding checklist can reduce friction and drive users closer to engagement and activation, ultimately moving the business closer to its retention goals.

4.2 Tools and Techniques for Mapping User Journeys: Making Every Interaction Count

Mapping user journeys requires a set of structured tools that help capture, analyze, and validate each interaction within the journey. These tools are instrumental in revealing where and how value is being delivered, ensuring that each interaction drives the business closer to its goals. By combining **hands-on techniques** for organizing journey data with **collaborative techniques** that build alignment across teams, businesses can create a unified vision that spans every level of the journey.

Hands-On Techniques

1. Persona Development
Personas are detailed, data-driven representations of user archetypes. They provide context for who the users are, their needs, motivations, and pain points. In user journey mapping, personas help align each stage with the real-life behaviors and expectations of the target audience, making it easier to design interactions that resonate and drive value.

Example: E-Commerce Personas

For an e-commerce site, a persona might represent a time-strapped working parent. Knowing that this persona values speed and convenience, designers can create a journey that prioritizes efficient search options, a simple checkout process, and rapid delivery. By mapping the journey with this persona in mind, every interaction—from homepage recommendations to checkout flow—becomes tailored to the user's needs, increasing satisfaction and driving sales.

2. Journey Mapping

Journey mapping is the process of outlining the specific steps users take when interacting with a product or service. It includes identifying touchpoints, pain points, and moments of delight, enabling businesses to see the experience from the user's perspective and find opportunities for improvement.

Example: Travel Booking Journey

For a travel booking platform, journey mapping might reveal friction points in the booking confirmation process. Users may feel unsure about their booking details or have trouble finding essential information. By enhancing these touchpoints—through clearer confirmation pages and real-time alerts—the platform creates a more reassuring experience, reducing user anxiety and increasing customer loyalty.

3. Touchpoint Analysis

Touchpoint analysis focuses on each point where the user interacts with the product. Each touchpoint is an opportunity to add value and strengthen the connection to the larger business objectives. Analyzing these interactions helps teams refine specific actions to ensure that each one contributes positively to the user journey.

Example: Mobile Banking App

A mobile banking app might analyze touchpoints such as balance checks, fund transfers, and loan applications. If the analysis shows that users are frequently abandoning fund transfers midway, the bank can make adjustments—like simplifying the transfer process or improving interface intuitiveness. These adjustments move the business closer to its goals of user satisfaction and increased transaction frequency.

Collaborative Techniques

1. Empathy Mapping

Empathy mapping brings teams together to better understand the thoughts, feelings, and motivations of users. This exercise fosters a deeper connection between teams and the end-users, ensuring that everyone involved in the design process shares a common perspective on user needs.

Example: Healthcare Service Provider

In a healthcare setting, empathy mapping might reveal that patients feel anxious about accessing their medical records online. By working collaboratively to address this insight, the design team and the IT department can prioritize features like secure login options, user-friendly interfaces, and clear explanations, all of which contribute to a more reassuring patient experience.

2. Stakeholder Workshops

Stakeholder workshops bring together representatives from multiple departments—design, marketing, customer service, engineering—to align on the journey's objectives. These sessions ensure that everyone understands the user journey's importance and how their role contributes to the broader goal.

Example: Telecom Company Redesigning Support Channels

For a telecom company improving its customer support journey, stakeholder workshops might reveal disconnects between departments. Customer service might be handling repeated issues that marketing and engineering teams weren't aware of. By discussing these pain points collaboratively, the teams can realign efforts to streamline the support experience, aligning with the overarching goal of reducing support inquiries and improving satisfaction.

4.3 Maximizing Business Value Through Detailed Interaction Mapping

Mapping each touchpoint in detail allows businesses to see how every interaction, however minor, contributes to or detracts from the strategic goals. This granular approach helps organizations validate each phase, ensuring that each interaction contributes incremental value toward the end goal.

Example Scenarios:

- **E-Commerce Checkout Process:** For an online retailer, each step in the checkout process represents an opportunity to either reinforce the user's decision to purchase or introduce friction that could lead to cart abandonment. By mapping this process in detail, the retailer can identify which stages create frustration, like entering payment information or confirming the order, and optimize them for faster conversions and reduced abandonment.
- **Hotel Booking Journey for Luxury Hospitality:** A luxury hotel chain might map the journey from booking to post-stay follow-up. Small details—such as personalized emails, easy-to-find booking confirmation details, and the ability to customize room preferences—enhance the guest experience and build loyalty. In the hospitality industry, these incremental improvements contribute to an overall sense of value and exclusivity, aligning with the brand's premium positioning.

Detailed interaction mapping provides traceability, allowing teams to revisit and refine each step. It also ensures that improvements are measured against strategic KPIs, linking tactical changes to overarching business objectives.

4.4 Leveraging Journey Mapping for Problem Definition and Validation

One of the most powerful aspects of journey mapping is its ability to serve as a foundation for understanding, defining, and validating problems. By breaking down each stage of the journey, teams can pinpoint the exact sources of friction, uncover unmet user needs, and build alignment around how to address these issues. Journey mapping also allows for **traceability** , which makes it easy to connect tactical-level interactions back to strategic goals, ensuring that all changes are meaningful and measurable.

Techniques for Defining and Validating Problems

1. Problem Definition Workshops

These workshops bring cross-functional teams together to identify and prioritize user problems. Journey maps provide a reference for these discussions, helping teams clearly articulate the problem, its impact, and potential solutions.

Example: Customer Support in Retail

For a retail company, a journey map might reveal that customers frequently contact support due to unclear return policies. In a problem definition workshop, teams can discuss this pain point, estimate its impact on customer satisfaction, and brainstorm solutions, such as clearer return instructions or a self-service return option. By addressing this issue, the company builds alignment around reducing support inquiries and improving user trust.

2. Value Mapping

Value mapping focuses on identifying which parts of the journey deliver the most value and which areas detract from it. By overlaying journey maps with value metrics (e.g., conversion rates, customer satisfaction scores), teams can validate which stages are meeting business objectives and which require further refinement.

Example: Airline Booking Experience

An airline might use value mapping to understand where users face challenges in booking flights, such as selecting seats or managing upgrades. By linking journey stages to value metrics, the airline can identify which interactions need improvement to align with goals of reducing booking time and enhancing the user experience.

4.5 The Role of User Journeys in Organizing and Validating Value Delivery

User journeys don't only map out interactions; they validate that value is being delivered at every stage. Each stage and touchpoint is an opportunity to measure whether users are achieving the intended outcomes and if the experience aligns with the business's strategic objectives. This iterative validation process makes journey maps valuable tools for tracking progress toward long-term goals.

Example Scenarios:

- **Subscription-Based Services:** For a subscription service, journey mapping helps track user engagement and retention at critical touchpoints. If the map reveals that users are disengaging after the onboarding phase, this insight can direct teams to optimize onboarding and provide added resources for sustained engagement.
- **Service Design for Banks:** In a banking context, user journeys can validate service design choices across both digital and physical touchpoints, from ATM interactions to mobile banking. Each interaction should align with the bank's goal of simplifying financial management for users. Journey maps allow the bank to track progress toward this goal and make adjustments as needed, such as introducing faster deposit options or enhancing in-app bill pay features.

4.6 Conclusion: User Journeys as Strategic Roadmaps

Mapping user journeys transforms the experience design process into a strategic roadmap, linking every interaction with overarching business goals. By understanding the journey in depth, organizations can ensure that every stage and touchpoint drives measurable value, moving incrementally closer to the desired outcomes. Through journey mapping, businesses can validate their assumptions, organize value delivery, and continuously refine experiences to meet both user needs and business objectives.

As we proceed through the book, we'll explore additional methods for operationalizing journey maps, such as feedback loops, usability testing, and data analytics. These tools will further enhance your ability to use journey maps as dynamic, actionable blueprints that drive strategic alignment, tactical execution, and sustained growth.

Chapter 5: Creating a User-Centered Experience Design Strategy

Introduction: The Power and Potential of Experience-Led Strategy

An experience-led strategy is more than a design approach—it's a comprehensive, user-centered framework that connects high-level business objectives to each detail of the user's journey. Unlike technology-driven or purely business-centric strategies, experience-led strategies focus on creating value by aligning business goals with real user needs. This end-to-end approach ensures solutions that are intuitive, aligned, and meaningful for users, driving both immediate and long-term business success.

In this chapter, we'll explore the unique concepts behind an experience-led strategy, detailing how it not only provides tangible outcomes (like increased efficiency and adoption) but also cultivates soft values (like user alignment and excitement). We'll examine how empathy, WIIFM (What's In It For Me?), and change levers create a foundation for understanding, defining, and building solutions.

Through in-depth examples and scenarios, we'll illustrate the impact of an experience-led approach across different industries and show how it creates a seamless connection between strategy and tactical implementation.

5.1 What Makes Experience-Led Strategy Different?

Unlike traditional strategies, which often prioritize technical capabilities or business-driven goals, an experience-led strategy prioritizes the user experience at every phase of development. This approach centers on creating solutions that are meaningful to users while meeting strategic objectives, which ultimately enhances the efficiency and effectiveness of the final product.

Why Experience-Led Strategy Matters

An experience-led approach delivers value by focusing on how solutions will be received, used, and valued by end-users. This focus ensures that the product not only functions as intended but also resonates with users, making it more likely to be adopted, championed, and sustained in the long term. Experience-led strategies generate value at multiple levels:

- **Strategic Business Value:** Solutions built with an experience-led strategy contribute to higher user retention, increased satisfaction, and more substantial brand loyalty. Because user needs are considered from the outset, these solutions also have lower rates of rework, lower support requirements, and fewer costly post-launch adjustments.
- **Efficiency Gains:** Experience-led strategies reduce friction by ensuring alignment early on. As a result, projects experience fewer bottlenecks, faster decision-making, and smoother workflows across teams, leading to significant time and cost savings.

Example: E-commerce Platform Checkout Process
Imagine an e-commerce company launching a new checkout process. Without an experience-led strategy, the focus might be on simply reducing the number of steps in the process. This approach might technically meet efficiency goals, but it doesn't address the emotional and functional needs of users, such as the desire for clear payment options or a visible support button. The result is a process that's fast but frustrating, leading to high abandonment rates.
With an experience-led strategy, the company would first identify what users value in a checkout experience. Through journey mapping and empathy mapping, they discover that users need transparent pricing, a progress indicator, and readily accessible support. The redesigned checkout process now includes these features, leading to lower abandonment rates, increased conversions, and higher user satisfaction.

5.2 Core Components of an Experience-Led Strategy

An effective experience-led strategy is built on foundational components that ensure alignment, drive engagement, and create solutions that resonate with users. These components include empathy, WIIFM, alignment, and change readiness.

Empathy and WIIFM: Understanding and Motivating Users

Empathy and **WIIFM (What's In It For Me?)** are two pillars that enable teams to define problems accurately and design solutions that resonate deeply with users.

- **Empathy:** Empathy helps teams step into the users' shoes, gaining insights into their frustrations, aspirations, and emotional drivers. By understanding the emotional journey of users, designers can identify what users truly need, leading to more impactful and user-friendly solutions.
- **WIIFM:** The WIIFM principle ensures that each feature and interaction clearly communicates value to the user. It answers the question, "Why should the user care?" and ensures that each element of the experience aligns with what matters most to users.

Example: Healthcare App for Patients with Chronic Conditions
Consider a healthcare app designed for patients managing chronic illnesses. An experience-led approach would use empathy mapping to understand the unique challenges of these users, like medication schedules, frequent lab tests, and daily symptom tracking. WIIFM would then guide the design, framing each feature (such as reminders for medications or quick access to lab results) as directly valuable to the patient. The result is an app that not only meets functional requirements but also addresses the emotional burden of chronic illness, making users more likely to engage with and benefit from it.

Building Alignment and Change Readiness from the Start

Experience-led strategies foster alignment by engaging stakeholders early in the process and ensuring they are part of the journey from strategy to execution. This approach builds readiness for change across teams, enabling a smoother adoption process.

- **Alignment Workshops:** Alignment workshops bring stakeholders from different functions together to collaboratively define objectives and align on priorities. By involving teams across departments, the strategy gains support and ensures that everyone is working toward a shared vision, reducing the likelihood of rework and misalignment later on.

- **Change Levers:** Change levers are tools used to prepare users for the new experience, making the transition smoother and reducing resistance. These might include educational sessions, demos, phased rollouts, or ambassadors who champion the solution within the organization.

Example: CRM Rollout in a Global Corporation

A global company implementing a new CRM system would use alignment workshops to ensure that all relevant teams—sales, marketing, and customer support—are aligned on the goals and benefits of the new system. Change levers, such as pilot programs in specific regions and ambassador training, would prepare teams for the new system, creating excitement and reducing resistance. This experience-led approach increases adoption, shortens learning curves, and minimizes the need for extensive retraining.

5.3 Building High-Fit Solutions Through Experience-Led Strategy

High-fit solutions are those that seamlessly align with business objectives and meet user needs at every level. Experience-led strategies achieve this by using what we call the **economy of experience** , balancing strategic vision with detailed, user-centered tactics.

The Economy of Experience: Balancing Strategy and Tactics

The economy of experience concept holds that each tactical detail, no matter how small, should reinforce the strategic goals of the business. Every micro-interaction, feature, and design choice contributes to the overall experience, bringing users closer to a seamless engagement with the product.

Example: Subscription-Based Streaming Platform
For a streaming platform aiming to reduce churn, the economy of experience balances strategic goals (e.g., increasing subscription retention) with tactical details, like personalized recommendations and clear onboarding. The strategic aim is to create value for the user, but this is realized through numerous small interactions that encourage users to explore more content, discover new shows, and feel invested in the platform.

Embedding a Culture of Shared Values: Efficiency, Empathy, and WIIFM

An experience-led strategy instills a culture that prioritizes efficiency, empathy, and the WIIFM principle, creating a shared value system across the organization. This culture not only improves the design process but also aligns internal teams around a user-first mindset.

- **Efficiency in Alignment:** Efficiency is achieved by fostering early alignment, which minimizes the likelihood of bottlenecks, miscommunications, and rework. With clear goals and shared values, teams can make faster decisions, leading to a more efficient design and development process.
- **Empathy and WIIFM:** A culture rooted in empathy and WIIFM leads to solutions that resonate with users on a deeper level. This approach reduces the need for training and support, as users find the product intuitive and valuable from the outset.

Example: Collaborative Platform for a Multinational Organization
Imagine a multinational organization launching a new internal collaboration platform. By embedding WIIFM in every feature, such as easy document sharing, personalized dashboards, and streamlined communication tools, the platform meets user needs and fosters a sense of value. Efficiency is built in by aligning teams early, ensuring that the solution meets diverse requirements across departments.

5.4 End-to-End Change Enablement in Experience-Led Strategy

Experience-led strategies recognize that change doesn't end with the product launch. Successful adoption requires an end-to-end approach to change enablement that builds readiness, encourages advocacy, and reduces resistance.

Techniques for Change Enablement and Building Readiness

1. Phased Rollouts and Gradual Adoption
Phased rollouts allow users to gradually adapt to the new solution, providing feedback and making adjustments as necessary. This phased approach builds comfort and familiarity, ensuring that users feel confident in using the new product.
Example:
A company introducing a new enterprise resource planning (ERP) system might start with a phased rollout in a single department. As the team becomes comfortable with the system, it is gradually expanded to other departments, each benefiting from the learnings and improvements made in earlier phases.

2. Continuous Feedback Loops and Iterative Improvements
Feedback loops ensure that users have a voice in the ongoing development of the product. By listening to user input, teams can make iterative adjustments that enhance the experience and keep it aligned with both user needs and business goals.
Example:
In a new mobile banking app, regular feedback sessions reveal that users struggle to find certain features. By iterating on the design based on this feedback, the bank enhances usability and strengthens the customer relationship, leading to higher engagement and satisfaction.

3. Champion Programs and User Ambassadors
User ambassadors serve as advocates for the new product, promoting its value among their peers and reducing resistance. Ambassadors can provide insights, training, and motivation, making adoption smoother and more organic.
Example:
When a pharmaceutical company introduces a new data management tool, it identifies champions within each team to advocate for the product. These ambassadors help build excitement, answer questions, and provide ongoing support, which drives higher adoption and minimizes friction during the transition.

5.5 The Outcomes of Experience-Led Strategies: Business and User Value

Experience-led strategies yield a range of hard and soft outcomes, benefiting both the business and the users. Hard outcomes, like increased adoption and reduced rework, provide immediate returns on investment, while soft outcomes, such as alignment and excitement, contribute to long-term success.

Hard Outcomes: Efficiency, Adoption, and Reduced Rework

- **Higher Adoption Rates:** Solutions that prioritize user needs and emphasize WIIFM see higher adoption rates because users find them immediately valuable and easy to use. Higher adoption reduces the need for extensive training and troubleshooting.
- **Reduced Rework:** Experience-led strategies address user needs early in the process, minimizing the need for costly redesigns and patches. By aligning with user feedback from the outset, the final product is more resilient and adaptable to future needs.

Soft Outcomes: Alignment, Advocacy, and Enthusiasm

- **Increased Alignment:** An experience-led strategy creates alignment between departments, reducing friction and ensuring that everyone from design to marketing shares a common vision. This alignment fosters smoother workflows and a cohesive end product.
- **Advocacy and Enthusiasm:** By involving users and building empathy from the start, experience-led strategies cultivate excitement and advocacy among users. These advocates become champions who help promote the solution, making it more likely to gain traction and see sustained engagement.

Example: Education Platform Rollout
An education platform built with experience-led strategy saw high adoption rates due to its intuitive design and user-centered features. Teachers who felt invested in the design process became advocates, reducing training costs and making adoption seamless. The platform's design, guided by empathy and WIIFM, also led to

reduced support inquiries, as teachers found it easy to navigate and incorporate into their classrooms.

5.6 Conclusion: Experience-Led Strategy as the Optimal Approach for Lasting Success

An experience-led strategy isn't just one way to design solutions; it's the best way to create products that meet business goals, resonate with users, and foster long-term loyalty. By centering each phase on user needs, fostering alignment, and building readiness, experience-led strategies deliver value that extends far beyond launch.

As we move forward, we will explore additional methodologies to sustain and enhance the impact of experience-led strategies over time. With experience-led strategies, businesses don't just build products—they create experiences that define their brand, inspire loyalty, and achieve both immediate and enduring success.

Chapter 6: Starting Your Journey into Experience Design Strategy

Introduction: Shaping Your Career with Experience Design Strategy

Embarking on a journey into Experience Design (XD) Strategy is a transformative step that offers more than just new skills—it reshapes how you see your work, approach problem-solving, and create value for both users and businesses. Whether you're new to the field, transitioning from another role, or looking to incorporate XD principles into your current position, this chapter serves as a comprehensive guide to kick-starting your career with a user-centered, experience-driven perspective. Here, we will bring to life the key concepts introduced throughout the book, making them practical, actionable, and relatable through real-world examples, thought experiments, and exercises.

As you progress, you'll learn how to view your work through a human-centered lens, balancing user needs with strategic goals. This chapter serves as the bridge between theoretical concepts and real-world application, providing you with the tools and insights to make XD Strategy an essential part of your career transformation. Let's begin by revisiting the core principles of empathy, WIIFM (What's In It For Me?), and alignment, and learning how to apply them in ways that are both strategic and impactful.

6.1 Preparing for Your Journey in Experience Design Strategy

Experience Design Strategy requires a unique mindset that blends creativity, empathy, and strategic thinking. Transitioning into this field, or even incorporating its principles into your current role, begins with adopting a user-centric way of thinking and aligning it with business objectives.

Exercise: Reflection on User-Centricity and Business Goals

Thought Experiment
Consider a product, service, or workflow you interact with daily in your role. Write down the following:

- **User Perspective** : Identify the primary user(s) of this product or process. What might they want or need from it? What frustrations could they experience?
- **Business Perspective** : Now consider what the business needs from this product or process. What are the primary

business goals (e.g., efficiency, revenue generation, customer satisfaction) it is designed to achieve?

Compare the two perspectives. Where do they align, and where do they diverge? This exercise will help you see how user-centric and business-driven goals can both complement and challenge each other—an essential insight for creating experience-led solutions.

Example: Online Banking Experience

Imagine you work at a bank that's developing an online banking platform. From a **user perspective** , customers want quick, secure access to their accounts and easy ways to make transactions. From a **business perspective** , the bank wants to drive user engagement, increase digital adoption, and reduce branch dependency. When both perspectives are considered, features like one-click transfers, biometric login for security, and 24/7 virtual support emerge as solutions that satisfy user needs while aligning with business goals.

6.2 Core Principles Revisited: Bringing Empathy, WIIFM, and Alignment to Life

An experience-led approach is anchored in empathy, understanding the WIIFM factor for users, and achieving alignment across teams and stakeholders. Here, we'll revisit these principles and explore exercises to incorporate them into your thinking.

Empathy: The Foundation of Experience Design

Empathy allows you to connect with users on an emotional level, ensuring that your designs address real human needs. Empathy is about seeing beyond functionality to understand how users feel, think, and behave when interacting with a product or service.

- **Empathy Mapping Exercise** : Choose a product or service you recently used, such as a mobile app, website, or even a customer service experience. Reflect on and write down what you think the designers assumed about the users' feelings, motivations, and frustrations. How would an empathy map have helped refine this experience?

Example: Fitness Tracking App

In a fitness tracking app, empathy mapping might reveal that users feel insecure about meeting their fitness goals and need frequent encouragement. Understanding this allows the design team to add motivational prompts and celebrate small milestones, enhancing user engagement and satisfaction.

WIIFM: The Power of What's In It For Me?

WIIFM (What's In It For Me?) is a crucial principle for ensuring that solutions provide clear value to users. WIIFM reminds you to continuously ask: "How does this benefit the user?" Solutions that clearly convey value are far more likely to drive adoption and satisfaction.

- **WIIFM Thought Experiment** : Think of a recent project in your role. List three features or aspects of the project. For each one, answer the WIIFM question from the user's perspective. This will help you identify areas where user value is clear and areas where it may need to be reinforced.

Example: Employee Collaboration Tool

Imagine your team developed a new collaboration tool for employees. One feature might allow for instant project updates. The

WIIFM for employees is clear: it saves them from chasing down updates manually, reducing workload and streamlining communication.

Alignment: Creating Shared Vision and Goals

Alignment is the process of ensuring that all stakeholders and teams share a common understanding of objectives and success criteria. Achieving alignment prevents misunderstandings, minimizes rework, and keeps projects on track.

- **Alignment Workshop Simulation** : Imagine you're leading a workshop with team members from different departments. Create an agenda where each team member shares their perspective on the project goals and key metrics. What potential conflicts might arise, and how could you address them to ensure everyone is aligned?

Example: Customer Service Platform for a Retail Brand
In a retail company, an alignment workshop for a new customer service platform might reveal differing goals among sales, support, and marketing. Sales may prioritize up-sell capabilities, while customer support focuses on reducing call times. By understanding these perspectives, the team can design a platform that balances quick service with opportunities for product recommendations.

6.3 Tools and Techniques: Building Your Experience Design Toolkit

To begin applying experience design, you'll need a toolkit of methods that help structure, analyze, and implement user-centered strategies. Here are the key tools and techniques for building a strong foundation in XD Strategy.

Journey Mapping: A Blueprint for User Experiences

Journey mapping allows you to visualize the user's experience from start to finish, capturing each interaction, emotion, and friction point along the way. This tool is essential for identifying where improvements can be made to drive both user satisfaction and business value.

- **Journey Mapping Exercise** : Take a product or service you interact with regularly, such as online shopping or using a mobile banking app. Sketch out a journey map of your own experience, listing each step, touchpoint, and any pain points you encounter. How might improvements at specific stages change your experience?

Example: E-commerce Checkout Process
In an e-commerce checkout journey, mapping each step—browsing, adding items to the cart, entering shipping info, confirming payment—can reveal friction points, like overly complex payment forms or hidden shipping costs. By identifying and addressing these issues, you can streamline the experience, reducing cart abandonment rates and increasing conversions.

Rapid Prototyping and Usability Testing: Testing and Validating Ideas Quickly

Prototyping and usability testing allow you to explore design ideas and gather feedback before full-scale implementation. Rapid prototyping lets you test concepts early, while usability testing validates these concepts with real users.

- **Prototyping and Testing Exercise** : Choose a feature from your current role that you believe could be improved. Sketch a simple prototype and test it with a colleague, asking for feedback. This exercise shows how early feedback can lead to meaningful design improvements.

Example: Internal Knowledge Management System
Imagine an internal knowledge management system where employees struggle to find documents. By prototyping a simpler, keyword-based search and testing it with a few team members, you can quickly identify whether this approach improves search efficiency before investing in full development.

6.4 Human-Centered Change: Building Readiness and Advocacy

A major component of successful experience design is ensuring that users are ready and excited to embrace new solutions. Experience-led strategies naturally build change readiness and advocacy by involving users early, aligning solutions with their needs, and cultivating champions.

Creating Change Readiness: Phased Rollouts and Feedback Loops

Change readiness is about ensuring that users are prepared and enthusiastic for new solutions. Phased rollouts and feedback loops are two techniques that help teams manage change effectively.

- **Change Readiness Thought Experiment** : Think of a recent change in your workplace. Consider the steps taken to introduce the change. Were users prepared? Were there feedback opportunities? Reflect on how a phased approach or feedback loop might have improved the process.

Example: New HR System in a Corporate Environment
When a company introduces a new HR system, phased rollouts might begin with the HR team before expanding to all employees. Feedback loops allow employees to report issues early, helping the team fine-tune the system before the full launch, reducing frustrations and ensuring a smoother transition.

Cultivating Advocacy: Leveraging Champions to Drive Adoption

Advocacy involves users who are invested in the success of the new solution and willing to promote it to their peers. Identifying and training ambassadors creates a built-in support system that drives adoption and reduces the need for extensive training.

- **Advocacy Exercise** : Identify potential ambassadors in your own role—colleagues who are excited about innovation or who are natural leaders. Think about how involving them early in new projects could help promote change among the team.

Example: New Communication Tool in a Remote-First Company
In a remote-first company adopting a new communication tool, choosing team leads as ambassadors can create advocates who help answer questions, share best practices, and build excitement, resulting in quicker adoption and higher engagement across the organization.

6.5 Moving from Strategy to Execution: Building Solutions with High Fit

Solutions developed with experience design strategy are not only aligned with business objectives but also resonate deeply with users. By balancing high-level strategic vision with tactical details, experience design creates high-fit solutions that meet immediate needs while supporting long-term goals.

The Economy of Experience: Balancing Strategy and Tactics

The economy of experience is about achieving the right balance between strategic objectives and tactical details. Every decision, feature, and interaction should reinforce the larger goal, making the solution feel both purposeful and cohesive.

- **Economy of Experience Thought Exercise** : Take a project you're involved in and identify one strategic goal and one tactical improvement. Reflect on how the tactical element contributes to the overall strategy. How could changes to the tactical level better support the strategic vision?

Example: Digital Transformation in a Retail Chain
For a retail chain undergoing digital transformation, a strategic goal might be to enhance customer loyalty. Tactically, the design team could add features to the loyalty app, such as personalized rewards and real-time offers. Each feature reinforces the larger strategy of encouraging repeat visits and deepening customer relationships.

6.6 Exercises and Thought Experiments to Solidify Your Experience Design Mindset

Throughout this chapter, we've discussed tools, principles, and techniques that form the backbone of experience design strategy. Below are additional exercises to help you apply these concepts in a way that directly benefits your current role and future career.

Thought Experiment: Mapping Your Career Journey

Imagine your career as a user journey. Identify key stages, such as early roles, pivotal moments, and future goals. What have been the major touchpoints? What pain points or challenges did you face? This exercise will help you view your career as a journey, highlighting the value of each step and identifying areas for improvement.

Exercise: Redesigning a Process in Your Current Role

Identify a recurring task or process in your current role that feels inefficient or cumbersome. Apply XD principles by mapping the journey of this process, pinpointing friction points, and reimagining it with empathy and WIIFM in mind. Consider who the "users" of this process are (e.g., teammates, clients) and think about ways to streamline or add value.

6.7 Conclusion: Your Journey Begins Here

Starting a career in Experience Design Strategy is more than just mastering tools and techniques—it's about adopting a mindset that places the user at the heart of every decision while aligning with broader business goals. By integrating empathy, WIIFM, and alignment into your daily work, you can begin transforming both your career and the impact you make within your organization.
As you prepare to move into the next chapter, remember that experience design is an evolving practice. The journey ahead will introduce advanced methods for measuring and optimizing your impact, showing you how to sustain alignment with both user needs and business objectives over time. This journey has just begun, and by embracing an experience-led approach, you're already laying the foundation for a career that combines creativity, strategy, and meaningful human connection.

Chapter 7: Building Your Path Forward with Experience Design Strategy

Introduction: The Journey Continues

As you reach the final chapter of this book, you've gained a solid foundation in Experience Design (XD) Strategy. You've learned how to apply principles of empathy, alignment, and strategic vision to create impactful, user-centered solutions that align with business goals. Now, it's time to turn this knowledge into action, making experience design not just a set of techniques but a core aspect of your career and a lens through which you see the world.

This chapter serves as both a summary and a launchpad. We'll revisit the essential hard and soft skills required in XD Strategy, discuss practical ways to apply these skills immediately, and encourage you to take a reflective look at your own strengths and growth areas. Here, you'll find exercises and thought experiments to help you internalize these principles, along with insights on how to steer your career in a direction that builds value for you, your team, and your organization. This chapter aims to set you on a path where XD Strategy becomes a part of who you are as a professional, a guiding compass as you shape your career and create experiences that resonate and inspire.

7.1 Reflecting on Hard and Soft Skills in Experience Design

Success in Experience Design Strategy requires a unique blend of technical and interpersonal skills, each playing a vital role in driving impactful outcomes. Let's break down the key hard and soft skills that form the backbone of an effective XD strategist and discuss how they complement each other.

Hard Skills: The Technical Tools of Experience Design

Hard skills are the foundational tools and techniques that allow you to build, test, and validate user-centered solutions. Mastery of these

tools enables you to conduct user research, map journeys, prototype solutions, and analyze data—all essential for creating experiences that are both intuitive and strategically aligned.
Key Hard Skills:

- **Journey Mapping:** A foundational skill, journey mapping enables you to visualize the user's experience, capture key touchpoints, and identify areas for improvement. As a practical tool, it ensures that every interaction aligns with user expectations and business objectives.
- **Prototyping and Usability Testing:** Prototyping allows you to bring ideas to life, while usability testing ensures those ideas meet user needs. Both skills require a commitment to iteration and feedback, as they involve testing assumptions, gathering data, and refining solutions based on real user interactions.
- **Data Analysis and Metrics Tracking:** Experience design is as much about numbers as it is about intuition. Skills in data analysis help you assess the effectiveness of your designs, measure key metrics (like engagement, retention, and satisfaction), and make data-informed decisions to drive continuous improvement.

Exercise: Skill Self-Assessment in Hard Skills
List each hard skill you've learned in this book and rate your proficiency on a scale of 1 to 5. For skills with lower scores, outline specific steps to improve—such as finding online courses, seeking mentorship, or practicing on small projects within your current role.
Example:
If you rate yourself lower in usability testing, you might plan to improve by conducting informal usability tests with colleagues or friends, seeking feedback, and learning from practical application. Over time, these exercises will build your confidence and competency in testing user-centered solutions.

Soft Skills: The Human Side of Experience Design

Soft skills—such as empathy, communication, and adaptability—are the qualities that enable you to connect with users, collaborate with teams, and navigate the complexities of change. They create a bridge between the technical aspects of design and the people who will use and benefit from your solutions.

Key Soft Skills:

- **Empathy and Active Listening:** Empathy allows you to see the world through the user's eyes, while active listening enables you to capture nuanced feedback. Together, they help you uncover underlying motivations and design experiences that resonate emotionally.
- **Collaboration and Alignment Building:** XD Strategy is rarely a solo effort. Strong collaboration skills allow you to build alignment across teams, departments, and stakeholders, ensuring that everyone is moving toward shared goals.
- **Adaptability and Resilience:** Experience design is an iterative process that often involves unexpected challenges. Adaptability and resilience allow you to respond to feedback, pivot when necessary, and continuously improve solutions without losing sight of the strategic vision.

Exercise: Reflecting on Soft Skills in Experience Design
Identify two to three soft skills you feel confident in and two to three areas where you see room for growth. For each growth area, write down ways to practice and improve. For example, if you want to improve empathy, consider observing real user interactions in your daily environment, taking note of subtle behaviors, frustrations, and motivations.

Example:
If alignment building is an area of growth, you might set a goal of initiating more cross-functional meetings in your current role, fostering open discussions with other teams to ensure shared understanding and collective buy-in.

7.2 Applying Experience Design Principles to Your Current Role

Whether you're aiming to become an XD strategist or simply want to incorporate experience design principles into your current position, the skills and concepts from this book can be applied right away. Below, we explore ways to bring these principles to life in a way that complements and elevates your work.

Human-Centered Innovation in Daily Work

Start by viewing every task through a human-centered lens. Ask yourself how each action, decision, or feature impacts the user experience and consider ways to enhance it. By embedding empathy and user focus into everyday work, you'll make experience design an integral part of your approach.

- **Exercise: Daily User Impact Check**
  Before beginning a new task, ask yourself, "How will this benefit the user?" Consider any opportunities to increase clarity, reduce friction, or add value from the user's perspective. This quick exercise builds the habit of centering users in everything you do.

Example: Improving Internal Communications
If you're responsible for internal communications, think about how employees experience the messages you send. Are they clear? Are they accessible? Could visual aids or simplified language improve understanding? By making small user-centered adjustments, you can improve engagement and build a more supportive work environment.

Leveraging Alignment and Collaboration to Drive Results

Experience design is most effective when teams are aligned and working cohesively. As you bring XD principles into your role, focus on building alignment by actively involving others, sharing insights, and seeking input.

- **Exercise: Alignment Workshop Simulation**
  Imagine you're leading a workshop for a cross-functional team. Prepare a plan where each member shares their goals and key metrics. Identify potential areas of conflict or misalignment and brainstorm ways to build consensus.

Example: Collaborative Product Development
In a product development role, bringing designers, developers, and marketers together early on can ensure that the product vision is shared across teams. By discussing user needs, potential challenges, and each team's contributions, you'll create a more cohesive product and reduce costly adjustments later on.

7.3 Moving Forward: Building a Career with Experience Design Strategy

As you look toward the next steps in your career, consider how experience design strategy can elevate your contributions and create new opportunities. By cultivating both hard and soft skills, applying XD principles to your current work, and continuously seeking growth, you'll be well-positioned to make a lasting impact.

Identifying Your Strengths and Areas for Growth

As you begin to apply experience design principles, it's essential to develop a pragmatic view of your strengths and areas for improvement. By understanding where you excel and where you can grow, you'll be able to focus your energy effectively and set realistic goals for career advancement.

- **Exercise: Career Reflection and Goal Setting**
  List three strengths that align with XD Strategy and three areas for growth. For each area of growth, create an action plan with specific, measurable steps. Revisit this plan regularly to assess your progress and adjust as needed.

Example:
If journey mapping is a strength, consider finding opportunities to lead journey mapping sessions in your organization, reinforcing your skill and showcasing your capabilities. For a growth area like collaboration, set a goal of co-leading a project with another team, focusing on open communication and alignment.

Creating a Personalized Development Plan

With a clear understanding of your strengths and growth areas, you can create a personalized development plan to deepen your skills and expand your experience design toolkit. A structured plan allows you to progress at a pace that fits your career goals while consistently building value for yourself and your organization.

- **Development Plan Structure** : Divide your plan into short-term (3–6 months), medium-term (6–12 months), and long-term (1–3 years) goals. Identify resources, mentors, and practical applications for each skill you want to develop.

Example: Development Plan for a Transitioning Professional
If you're transitioning into experience design from another field, your short-term goals might include taking online courses on journey mapping and prototyping. Medium-term goals could involve seeking mentorship and volunteering for user-centered projects. Long-term goals might include leading experience design initiatives or integrating XD principles into strategic decision-making at your organization.

7.4 Thought Experiments and Practical Exercises to Solidify Your Skills

Throughout this chapter, we've explored exercises and thought experiments to help you internalize XD Strategy concepts. Here are additional activities to reinforce these skills and encourage continuous learning.

Thought Experiment: Mapping Your Career as a User Journey

Visualize your career journey from the perspective of a user journey map. Identify key stages, achievements, challenges, and turning points. Think about where you are now, your long-term goals, and the touchpoints that could move you closer to them. This exercise helps you see your career as an evolving experience, allowing you to apply XD principles to your own growth.

- **Prototyping and Testing Exercises** : Remember to integrate prototyping and usability testing into your design process regularly. Each prototype is an opportunity to learn, iterate, and refine, ensuring that your solutions are intuitive and meet the user's needs.

Example Reflection : Reflect on a recent design process where journey mapping or prototyping shaped the outcome. How did these tools help you see things from the user's perspective? How might you apply these techniques in future projects to improve alignment and user satisfaction?

Moving Forward: Applying Experience Design Strategy to Your Career

With a strong foundation in Experience Design Strategy, you're ready to apply these concepts to your current role or new opportunities. This book is part of a larger journey and serves as a stepping stone to more advanced strategies and applications covered in the upcoming books in this series. By applying these foundational concepts, you'll create meaningful experiences that foster user loyalty, build strategic alignment, and contribute to long-term business success.

Developing a Career Built on Empathy, Strategy, and Innovation

As you continue to grow in your career, keep in mind that Experience Design Strategy is both a skill set and a mindset. The principles you've learned here—empathy, alignment, journey mapping, and user-centered design—are tools you can apply to any role, project, or industry. Embrace these principles as guiding values, ones that not only shape your work but also define how you interact with others, build relationships, and drive change.

- **Self-Reflection Exercise** : Take time to assess your strengths and areas for growth in both hard and soft skills. Use the exercises in Chapter 7 to create a career development plan, setting achievable goals to refine your skills and expand your knowledge of experience design.

Immediate Application: Putting XD Strategy into Practice

Start applying XD Strategy concepts right away, even in small ways. Use journey mapping to improve existing processes, hold alignment workshops to clarify team goals, and practice empathy mapping to ensure that user needs remain at the center of your decisions.

- **Practical Experiment** : Choose a project or task in your current role and apply one XD Strategy technique to enhance it. For example, if you're improving a process, create a journey map to visualize the user's experience. If you're developing a new feature, build a low-fidelity prototype and gather feedback from users or colleagues. Small experiments like these will solidify your understanding and build confidence in your ability to apply XD Strategy effectively.

Looking Ahead: The Next Step in Your Experience Design Journey

This book is only the beginning. As you continue to develop your expertise in Experience Design Strategy, the next books in this series will explore advanced techniques for operationalizing XD across entire organizations, scaling user-centered design in complex environments, and leveraging XD as a tool for business transformation.

Upcoming Topics in the Series :

- **Advanced Operationalization of XD** : Explore methods for integrating XD Strategy across teams, aligning departments, and embedding user-centered practices into the company's DNA.
- **Scaling User-Centered Design** : Learn techniques for expanding XD practices in larger organizations, ensuring consistency and maintaining quality as you scale.
- **Experience Design as a Driver of Business Transformation** : Discover how to use experience design principles to drive organizational change, elevate brand value, and create sustainable competitive advantages.

With each book, you'll deepen your knowledge, refine your skills, and learn how to make experience design an integral part of your career. The journey you've started here will continue to evolve, equipping you with the tools and insights to become a leader in experience design.

Final Thoughts: The Value of Experience Design Strategy in Your Career

Experience Design Strategy isn't just a methodology—it's a way of creating value, solving problems, and making a positive impact on users, teams, and businesses. As you apply these principles, you'll find that XD Strategy enhances not only the solutions you create but also your approach to challenges, your interactions with others, and your career trajectory.

By placing the user at the heart of your work, balancing empathy with strategic objectives, and constantly iterating for improvement, you're building a skill set that is both highly valuable and personally rewarding. Remember that every project is an opportunity to practice and refine your skills, and each experience will bring you closer to becoming a skilled, user-centered strategist.

Thank you for taking this journey through Experience Design Strategy. Embrace the principles, continue learning, and let your work speak for itself. With this foundation, you're equipped to create experiences that are not only impactful but transformative—driving success for users, teams, and organizations alike. Here's to a fulfilling and innovative journey ahead.

www.ingramcontent.com/pod-product-compliance
Lightning Source LLC
LaVergne TN
LVHW051748050326
832903LV00029B/2799

* 9 7 9 8 3 4 5 8 3 9 2 5 6 *